French Guiana
Memory Traces of the Penal Colony

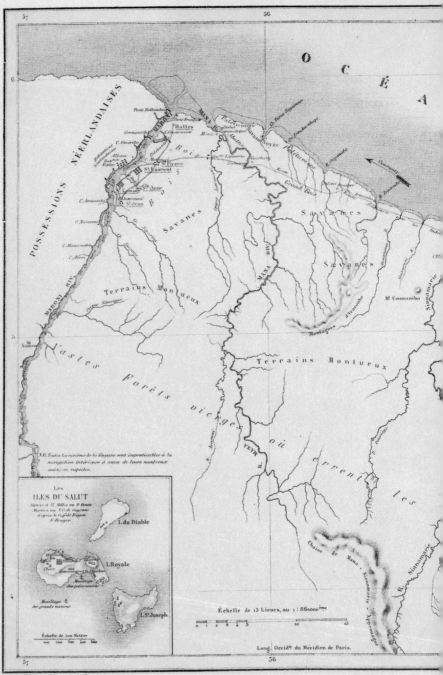

6

O C É A

POSSESSIONS NÉERLANDAISES

Poste Hollandais

Hattes

Cormontibo   C. Simirbec

C. Marian   St. Pierre
St. Laurent

Louisa   St. Anne
C. Aroumata   R. St. Jean

C. Batavens

C. Manawabira

C. Acres

MARONI RIV.

Bois

Savanes

Savanes

Savanes

Terrains Montueux

MANA RIV.

Montagnes d'Iracoubo

Mt. Coumanibo

5

L'astes   Forêts   vierges   où   errent   les

Terrains   Montueux

VSYR R.

N.B. Toutes les rivières de la Guyane sont impraticables à la
navigation intérieure à cause de leurs nombreux
sauts ou rapides.

Chaîne   de   Mana - Sinnamarie - Approuague

Les
ILES DU SALUT
Situées à 27 Milles ou 9 lieues
Marines au N.O. de Cayenne
d'après le Cap.ne Projeté
F. Bouyer

I. du Diable

I. Royale

Commandant & St. Charbon

Mouillage
des petits navires

Mouillage
des grands navires

I. St. Joseph

Échelle de 500 Mètres
100   200   300   400   500

Échelle de 15 Lieues, au 1:860000.eme

0 1 2 3 4 5   10   15

Long. Occid.le du Méridien de Paris.

Grave chez Erhard 11 r. Duguay Trouin - Paris.

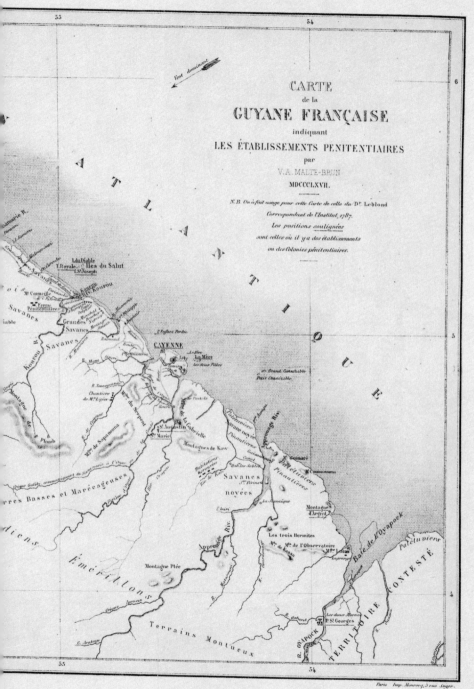

French Guiana, showing penitentiary establishments

French Guiana
Memory Traces of the Penal Colony

—✳—

PATRICK CHAMOISEAU

—✳—

Photographs by

RODOLPHE HAMMADI

—✳—

TRANSLATED BY MATT REECK

WESLEYAN UNIVERSITY PRESS

Middletown, Connecticut

Wesleyan University Press
Middletown CT 06459
www.wesleyan.edu/wespress

Designed by Richard Hendel
Typeset in Quadraat by Tseng Information Systems, Inc.

Library of Congress Cataloging-in-Publication Data
Names: Chamoiseau, Patrick, author. | Hammadi, Rodolphe, 1958– photographer. |
Reeck, Matt, translator.
Title: French Guiana : memory traces of the penal colony / Patrick Chamoiseau ;
photographs by Rodolphe Hammadi ; translated by Matt Reeck.
Other titles: Guyane. English
Description: Middletown : Wesleyan University Press, 2020. | Includes bibliographical
references. | Summary: "A translation of the collaborative work Guyane: Traces-mémoires
du bagne, by the Martinican writer Patrick Chamoiseau and the German-Algerian
photographer Rodolphe Hammadi" — Provided by publisher.
Identifiers: LCCN 2019053818 (print) | LCCN 2019053819 (ebook) |
ISBN 9780819579300 (trade paperback) | ISBN 9780819579317 (ebook)
Subjects: LCSH: Prisons—French Guiana—History. |
Prisons—French Guiana—History—Pictorial works.
Classification: LCC HV9615.7 .C4813 2020 (print) |
LCC HV9615.7 (ebook) | DDC 365/.9882—dc23
LC record available at https://lccn.loc.gov/2019053818
LC ebook record available at https://lccn.loc.gov/2019053819

5 4 3 2 1

Maps: Carte de la Guyane française indiquant les établissements pénitentiaires,
1Fi50, used with permission of the Archives territoriales de Guyane; Îles du Salut,
14DFC 1054B, used with permission of the Archives nationales d'outre-mer.

Contents

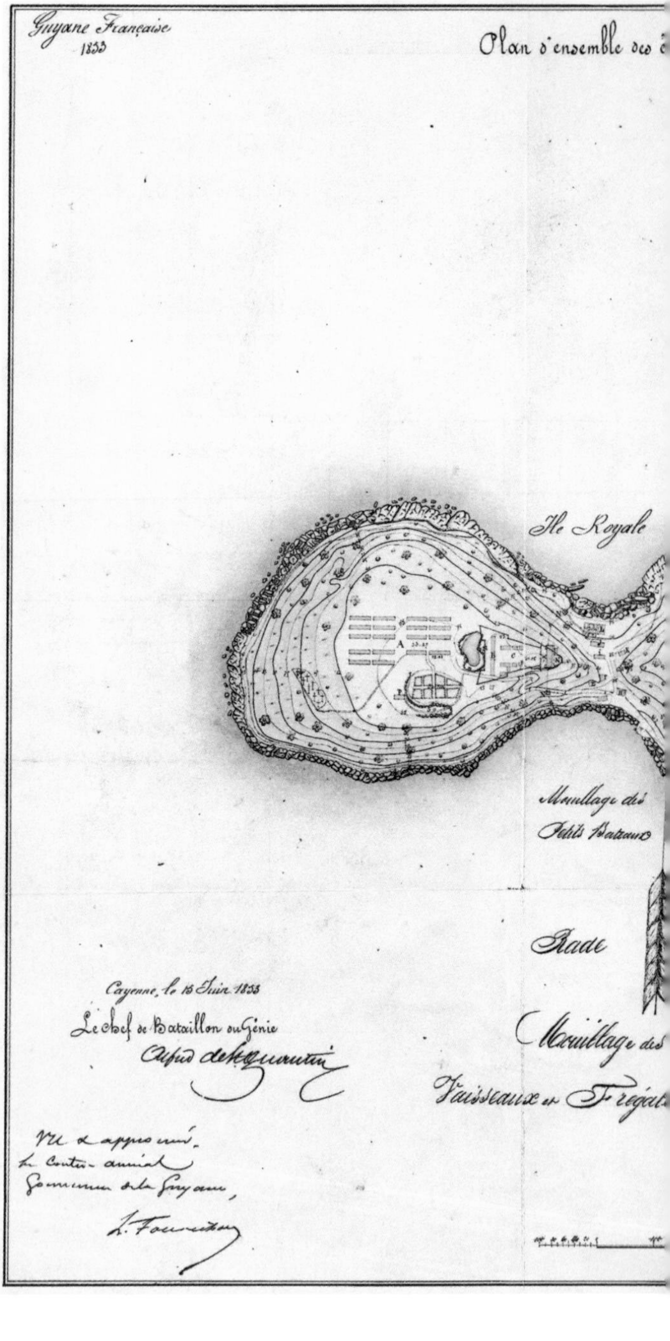

Guyane Française
1853

Plan d'ensemble des é

Île Royale

Mouillage des
Petits Bateaux

Rade

Mouillage des
Vaisseaux et Frégates

Cayenne, le 15 Juin 1853

Le Chef de Bataillon au Génie
Alfred de Kerquantin

Vu et approuvé.
Le Contre-amiral
Gouverneur de la Guyane,

L. Fournier

Salvation's Islands

Île du Diable

Légende
Île Royale

A	Camp des Transportés
B	Casernes provisoires
c	Établissemts divers
D	Corps-de-Garde
E	Commandant
F	Service de Santé
G	Caserne du milieu
H	Officiers
I J K	Magasins
L	Manutention
M	Caserne en construction
N...	Enceinte et Caserne défensive, projetée
O	Colonne Commémorative
P	Cuisine des transportés

Île St Joseph

1 à 3	Baraques pour 60 hommes
3	Caserne provisoire
4	Église et Logemt de l'aumônier
5	Logement des officiers
6	Cuisines

Nota : Le plan de Comparaison est à 100 mètres
au dessus des plus basses eaux.

Fort Laurent

Île St Joseph

Foreword

CHARLES FORSDICK

The absence of memorialization of the *bagne* is one of the most striking examples of postcolonial amnesia in the French-speaking world. Omitted—like most other locations relating to colonial expansionism—from Pierre Nora's *Realms of Memory* project (the seven volumes of which appeared between 1984 and 1992), the penal colony epitomizes the ways in which memories of colonial empire have been filtered, distorted, singularized, and often repressed. The *bagne* constituted nevertheless a carceral archipelago, a network of sites scattered across France itself (where prisons in the port cities of Brest, La Rochelle, and Toulon were complemented by penal colonies for young offenders), North Africa (location of the infamous "Biribi" or military prisons and forced labour camps), and elsewhere in the colonial empire (most notably French Guiana, New Caledonia and Vietnam).[1]

French Guiana had served as the destination for political dissidents during the French Revolution, but it was in 1854 that Napoleon III signed a decree relating to forced labour that turned the South American colony into a formal penitential destination for civil transportees from France and the wider French colonial empire.[2] (They would as a result of legislation in 1885 be joined also by recidivists, prisoners guilty of repeated petty crimes.) The logic and function of the penal colony were clear: on the one hand, it permitted the location far from France or other colonies of those considered politically and socially undesirable; on the other, it provided the workforce for the colonization of a country that had proved (and would continue to prove) stubbornly resistant to imperial expansionism and settlement. The conditions were harsh, for convicts, warders, and colonial administrators alike, even on the supposedly more salubrious Salvation's Islands where the impact of tropical diseases was reduced. Prisoners were moreover subject to a regime of *doublage*, meaning that convicts sentenced to less than eight years of hard labour were obliged to remain in French Guiana for a period equal to their original sentence whilst those sent for more than eight years were exiled for life.

The mortality rate was such that, from 1864, French metropolitan convicts were diverted to the newly established penal colony of New Caledonia. The *bagne* in the Pacific operated for little more than sixty years, with transportation to there ended in 1897 after only three decades. The penal colony in French Guiana continued to function throughout this time, receiving convicts from elsewhere in the French colonial empire. With the closure of the penal establishments in Melanesia, metropolitan prisoners were again dispatched to South America. A campaign of reform triggered by the work of investigative journalist Albert Londres in the 1920s led, however, to the passing of legislation in 1938 that formally ended penal transportation. Another key text, by the Guianese author and leading figure in the Negritude movement Léon-Gontran Damas, pointed to the failure of the *bagne*. *Retour de Guyane*, published in 1938, provided such an incendiary critique of the penitentiary and the colonial structures with which it was inextricably bound that the French Guianese authorities seized and destroyed as many copies of the book as they could. This was not, however, the end of the penal colony. French Guiana was under the control of Vichy in the first years of the Second World War, during which time the conditions under which convicts lived rapidly deteriorated—the former French Minister of Justice Robert Badinter went so far as to claim in 2017 that this treatment constituted a crime against humanity.[3] Repatriation of surviving French prisoners took place between 1946 and 1953, with some Algerian prisoners not returning to their country of origin until the early 1960s.

Unlike the penal colonies in Australia, the French Guianese *bagne* consequently remains a phenomenon of recent history, meaning that memory debates relating to it have much closer resonance with the present. It is telling, therefore, that the institution has been subject to progressive amnesia despite its everyday visibility in the built environment: many historic public buildings and much of the infrastructure in French Guiana were built with convict labour; whilst subject to processes of postcolonial ruination, other sites of the penal colony itself have persisted and it is these structures that form the focus of the book that follows.

French Guiana: Memory Traces of the Penal Colony is a hybrid work, a photo-essay in which text and image are juxtaposed in ways that are more suggestive and disruptive than prescriptive.[4] Patrick Chamoiseau's essay in which he elaborates the notion of the "memory trace" sits alongside a selection of photographs of various penal sites by Rodolphe Hammadi, a French photographer of German and Algerian heritage. The book appeared initially in modest paperback format, published in 1994 by the Caisse nationale des monuments historiques et des sites, in a collection entitled "Monuments en parole" devoted primarily to French metropolitan heritage locations such as Notre-Dame in Paris or the Grand Théâtre in Bordeaux. Chamoiseau's texts were republished in a more sumptuous coffee table version by Editions GANG in 2011, retitled *Bagne AP* and accompanied in this version by the photographs of Jean-Luc de Laguarigue. The volume initially appeared in the context of significant memory debates in France, focused not least around the bicentenary of the French Revolution in 1989. The place of the colonial past in these processes remains moot, despite the importance of the Caribbean colonies in seeking to link *liberté, égalité, fraternité* to a push (successfully, in the case of Saint-Domingue or Haiti) for universal emancipation from slavery.

In the early 1990s, when this book first appeared, the apparatus supporting penal heritage in French Guiana was limited, part of a more general process—which Chamoiseau himself identifies—that consigned the institution to oblivion. By then, there was already limited dark tourism to Salvation's Islands, sites administered since the 1960s by the Space Centre at Kourou in a striking juxtaposition of two radically different experimental projects.[5] Other key locations of the penal colony remained at the time underdeveloped, however, either subject to the encroachment of nature (as was the case with the so-called *bagne des annamites* at Montsinéry-Tonnegrand, built for Indochinese political dissidents in the 1930s) or serving as repurposed or inhabited heritage (strikingly the case with the Camp de la Transportation at Saint-Laurent du Maroni, still partly occupied—when Hammadi took his photographs—by refugees of Maroon origin exiled by neighbouring Suriname's civil war).[6] Chamoiseau is acutely aware, however, of dominant official memory practices, particularly those privileging colonial, political, and military officials evident in statues and plaques in French Guiana (the monument to abolition in Cayenne, showing the generous Victor Schoelcher granting the gift of freedom to a grateful formerly enslaved young boy is a classic illustration of this), and eclipsing persistent yet often silenced oral memories. He alludes at the same time to more informal processes of amnesia, not least the place of the penal colony in the popular imaginary, according to which convicts are associated with "celebrity" prisoners or at least seen exclusively as ethnically white.[7] His response is the search for alternative "memory traces," presented by Chamoiseau as "broken, diffused, scattered," but stubbornly discernible to those willing to look more closely and listen more attentively.

Hammadi's photographs cover a range of different sites: Alfred Dreyfus's dwelling on Devil's Island; the administrative and prison buildings on Royale Island; the overgrown cell blocks of the *bagne* on Saint-Joseph's Island; the remaining brick pillars of the Camp de la Forestière near Saint-Laurent du Maroni, accessible only with the aid of a machete and a knowledgeable local guide; Saint-Joseph's church at Iracoubo, decorated with the murals of convict Pierre Huguet. Together, these images reveal the dangers of reducing the word *bagne* to a single site (the French often misleadingly talk about the "bagne de Cayenne") or to a single history.

Chamoiseau describes his engagement with these places, his decipherment of graffiti and other faded inscriptions discovered in them, his interrogation of their silences, his affective response as suppressed memories emerge. The place of *French Guiana: Memory Traces of the Penal Colony* in Chamoiseau's wider *oeuvre* is significant. The author's interest in penal cultures is not limited to this text: the novel *Un dimanche au cachot* (2007) uses a palimpsestic understanding of space, for instance, to create links—through the story of its troubled young female protagonist—between an eighteenth-century cell for the enslaved and the children's home that occupies the site now.[8] This relationship between memory and the persistent traces of different cultures of incarceration is equally pertinent for the current text. *Memory Traces* appeared five years after the co-authored manifesto *In Praise of Creoleness*, a call for more active recognition of the cultural and linguistic heterogeneity of the French Antilles.[9] It was published only two years after the writer's novel *Texaco* had been awarded the Goncourt Prize.[10] The photo-essay on French Guiana continues the logic of those works, on the one hand by opening heritage debates up to the cultural and ethnic diversity underpinning creoleness, on the other by engaging in a recovery of those voices often systematically silenced by officially endorsed narratives of the past. His approach was to read the vestiges of the penal colony as evidence of ruination, a process explored by Ann Laura Stoler, who sees such a metaphor of the links between the colonial past and postcolonial present as preferable to more linear and common evocations of colonial legacy.[11] The ruin becomes organic, a reflection—through layers of moss, damp, soil, and dust—of the oblivion to which state-sanctioned memory appeared to have condemned the penal colony, but also a space of counter-memory, a repository of intersecting traces of the past—of "the histories of the dominated and demolished memories"—reactivated through the rhythms of the walking of the attentive wanderer who encounters them afresh. Steering away from the pitfalls of what is known increasingly as "ruin porn," Chamoiseau prefigures instead debates in contemporary heritage studies about the curation as opposed to the preservation of decay.[12] The radical heritage practice he proposes is one of poetic intervention by photographers, sculptors and artists.

A quarter of a century on, the sites of the French Guianese penal colony have benefited from major heritage initiatives: the encroachment of nature into the *bagne des annamites* has been partially reversed and the site turned into a heritage-cum-leisure destination; the Transportation Camp at Saint-Laurent du Maroni has been significantly restored, with the process of ruination partially stabilized to create an impressive museum, documentation centre, and living exhibition space. Chamoiseau's *Memory Traces* is a reminder that the conservation of such sites should reserve a place for creativity, for the imagination and for an openness to affective responses to the past. Such alternative forms of engagement, he argues, permit access to interstitial spaces, between the cracks of the ruin—it is from these that muffled, forgotten and otherwise marginalized voices will whisper back.

NOTES

1. On the global dimensions of penal colonies, see Clare Anderson (ed.), *Global History of Convicts and Penal Colonies* (London: Bloomsbury, 2018).

2. For an overview of penal transportation in the French colonial empire, see Stephen A. Toth, *Beyond Papillon: The French Overseas Penal Colonies 1854–1952* (Lincoln: University of Nebraska Press, 2006).

3. On the final years of the *bagne*, see Danielle Donet-Vincent, *La Fin du bagne* (Rennes: Éditions Ouest France, 1992). For Badinter's intervention, see "Le bagne de Guyane: un crime contre l'humanité," *Le Monde*, 24 November 2017.

4. See Andrew Stafford, "Patrick Chamoiseau and Rodolphe Hammadi in the penal colony. photo-text and memory-traces," *Postcolonial Studies*, 11.1 (2008), 27–38.

5. See Peter Redfield, *Space in the Tropics: From Convicts to Rockets in French Guiana* (Berkeley, CA: University of California Press, 2000).

6. See Christèle Dedebant and Céline Frémaux, *Le Bagne des Annamites: Montsinéry-Tonnegrande* (Cayenne: Le Service de l'Inventaire général du patrimoine culturel de la Région Guyane. 2012), and Clémence Léobal, "Politiques urbaines et recompositions identitaires en contexte postcolonial: les marrons à Saint-Laurent du Maroni (1975–2012)," rapport de recherche, Ministère de la Culture et de la Communication, 2014.

7. A key example is Henri Charrière, commonly known under his nickname "Papillon," whose autobiography was popularized in a memorable 1973 film version, starring Steve McQueen and Dustin Hoffman and directed by Franklin J. Schaffner (this was remade by Michael Noer in 2018); Chamoiseau's essay also alludes to the TV biopic of Guillaume Seznec screened in 1983, for whose filming part of the Transportation Camp had been restored.

8. Patrick Chamoiseau, *Un dimanche au cachot* (Paris: Gallimard, 2007).

9. Jean Bernabé, Patrick Chamoiseau and Raphaël Confiant, *Eloge de la créolité: édition bilingue français-anglais / In Praise of Creoleness* (Paris: Gallimard, 1993).

10. Patrick Chamoiseau, *Texaco*, trans. by Myriam Réjouis and Val Vinokurow (New York: Granta, 1997).

11. Ann Laura Stoler, *Duress: Imperial Durabilities in our Times* (Durham, NC: Duke University Press, 2016).

12. Siobhan Lyons (ed.), *Ruin Porn and the Obsession with Decay* (Basingstoke: Palgrave Macmillan, 2018). See also Caitlin Desilvey, *Curated Decay: Heritage beyond Saving* (Minneapolis: University of Minnesota Press, 2017).

Translator's Note

MATT REECK

When a person strives to learn another language, the dictionary is a solid friend. It presents language as a reliable, repeatable system. *This word*, it says, *means this*. For certain words, the dictionary traces out many nuances. But for such a word, a word with nuance, a word with as much connotation as denotation, does this tracing out of nuance in fact go far enough? The acknowledgment of some nuance would in turn suggest further nuance that the dictionary cannot include—cannot because the various senses, shades, and metaphorical extensions of certain words would then spill over countless pages, and the project of the dictionary—namely, the project of presenting language as a centralized, stable, and reliable force—would be thwarted.

Reading Patrick Chamoiseau brings this to mind. Chamoiseau is a poet writing in prose—a prose writer with a poet's sensibility. "I sacrifice everything to the music of the words," Linda Coverdale quotes him as saying in her introduction to *Slave Old Man*.[1] That words have sonorous qualities might mean that a translation of his work would, by his own attestation, be a homophonic one as much as one that attempts to map the meaning of one word in French onto the meaning of one word in English, ad infinitum. While these two rubrics, polarized in this exposition, outline the concerns of any literary translation, their tension is particularly intense in *French Guiana: Memory Traces of the Penal Colony*. On the one hand, there is music, and, on the other hand, there is the dictionary's meaning. The fact that *French Guiana: Memory Traces of the Penal Colony* also strives to be a theoretical, if creative, intervention in history adds necessarily to the text's complexity. If it would be possible for a text to be *half* poetic, *half* theoretical, and *half* historiographical, then this is that text—a text greater than a single text.

The Neologism of the Memory Trace

The title's neologism of a "Memory trace" signals the theoretical nature of Chamoiseau's literary project. Chamoiseau plainly borrows from the theoretical vocabulary of his fellow Martinican writer Édouard Glissant. Chamoiseau writes that, for Glissant, a trace has an essence that is "composite, fragile, uncertain." A trace is "floating."[2] Like Glissant, Chamoiseau does not propose theoretical neologisms as strictly rational, logical, or entirely consistent concepts. Writing about Glissant's uses of the phrase "Tout-monde" [All-world] and "l'identité-relation" [relational identity], Chamoiseau affirms that, for his fellow poet, "these are not what we might properly call "concepts"; rather they are " 'poe-concepts.' "[3] He goes on to say that Glissant's power derives from his ability to remain in "poetic indefinition"— a lack of definition that poetry espouses, promotes, or abides by. These comments describe Chamoiseau's *French Guiana: Memory Traces of the Penal Colony* as well, both in the author's desire to intercede in a conceptual arena and in his commitment to avoid the central problem of authoritative histories that his text addresses: how official documents, how official organs of state, and how state-sponsored histories control the very definition of reality. Chamoiseau's project of affective history in *French Guiana: Memory Traces of the Penal Colony* disavows such authoritative control and the empirical epistemology that it implies.

Chamoiseau's beliefs about the limitations of rational history writing, the limits of rational concepts, and the availability of literary strategies through which the writer can create alternative histories combine to result in the poetic nature of this neologism. Chamoiseau writes that a Memory trace "rises from forgetfulness, from the forgotten, from the impossible, from the dominated; and it bears witness in a horizontal manner, open, and multiple."[4] Chamoiseau suggests that a Memory trace, like any vestige, is only ever partial, itself but a single memory, a single moment, opening into a universe of memories whose full recording can never be achieved. Chamoiseau defines the term against "la Mémoire-une," itself a neologism. I translate this term as "Memory-One" so as to bring attention to its poetic-conceptual nature. Memory-One is "authorized memory," that which has to authority to "organize a collection of memories."[5] Memory-One is the sort of memory that history with a capital "h" writes—a memory, a history, which purports to be universal.

NOTES

1. Linda Coverdale, introduction to *Slave Old Man*, by Patrick Chamoiseau, translated by Linda Coverdale (New York: New Press, 2018), xiv.

2. Patrick Chamoiseau, *La matière de l'absence* (Paris: Éditions du Seuil, 2016), 130.

3. Ibid., 286–87.

4. Ibid., 347.

5. Ibid.

French Guiana

Memory Traces of the Penal Colony

To this lasting dream that keeps French Guiana in my heart.

PATRICK CHAMOISEAU

Immobile in front of the parade, here are the memorial Stones that no

marching order can touch or shake. They remain.

VICTOR SEGALEN

Cemetery Saint-Laurent du Maroni

Our Monuments remain like suffering.
They bear witness to suffering.
They preserve suffering.

They are the common types of structures produced by the colonial trajectory: forts, churches, chapels, mills, jails, buildings concerned with the exploitation of sugarcane slavery, structures of military occupation. Statues and marble plaques celebrate explorers and conquistadores, governors and elite administrators. In French Guiana, like in the Antilles, these structures don't inspire much affective response; if they bear witness to European colonials, they don't bear witness to other populations (Amerindians, African slaves, Hindu immigrants, Syrian-Lebanese, Chinese) that thrown onto colonial lands and, once there, had to find a way to survive, then to live together, and eventually to produce an original culture and identity.

The trajectory of these people was silenced. Not included in the colonial Chronicle, this trajectory came alive in their arts, their resistances, their heroisms, without stelai, without statues, without monuments, without documents. Only the word of the Elders that circulates beneath writing—oral memory—bears witness.

Yet a word doesn't make a monument.
A word doesn't make History.
A word doesn't make Memory.

A word transmits histories.

A word diffuses memories.

A word bears witness in traces, in reminiscences, in protean anecdotes where the imagination intermixes with feeling.

And with emotion.

That is why we often say that in the Americas, monuments (and History with a capital "h") bear witness to colonials, to the dominant power, to the colonial act with its genocides, enslavements, and assassinations of the Other. History, Memory, and the Monument magnify or exalt (from the top of their supremacy) the crime that the colonial Chronicle legitimated.

The creole peoples of the Americas are tormented by their stifled collective memory and their subterranean histories. When they turn to face the Monuments that define their spaces, they don't find themselves there. Or, through venerating these structures, they become enslaved by colonial Memory and History.

"Our landscape is its own monument: the trace that it signifies is detectable underneath. It's the sum total of history,"* wrote Édouard Glissant. This means that in the America of plantations (whether they be in French Guiana, on the edges of continents, or in the Antillean archipelago), in order to differentiate between the trajectories of the diverse peoples that are found there, it is necessary to reinvent the notion of the monument, to deconstruct the notion of patrimony. Beneath the texts of colonial History, it is necessary to find the trace of histories. Beneath the lofty Memory of forts and buildings, it is necessary to find the few places where, for these collectivities, the decisive stages were crystallized.

* Édouard Glissant, Le discours antillais (Paris: Éditions du Seuil, 1981).

[6]

Reading the Antillean landscape, Glissant detected the path of runaway slave resistances in the highlands that no writing (in script or in monument) witnessed: his reading of the coastal plains and inhabited spaces grants us original witnesses to the capitulations and crafty revolts that both slaves and immigrants learned to use in order to survive. His decoding of urban spaces allows us to follow (without pedestals and without statues) the slow progression of the former slaves toward the conquest of liberty. He marked out our *Memorial sites*, or more exactly the places of our *Memory traces*, whose symbolic, affective, and functional meanings, and whose known, evolving, and living significations, far outstrip the immobile purport of traditional monuments that we catalogue in Western Memory.

I, a creole American, sing histories against History.
I sing memories against Memory.
I sing Memory traces against the Monument.

The Diverse opposes the Unique
The open, the enclosed.

What is a Memory trace?

It's a space forgotten by History and by Memory-One, because it bears witness to the histories of the dominated and demolished memories, and it helps preserve them.

The Memory trace cannot be made manifest by a monument, by stelai, by statues, or by the cult of the document of our former historians.

The Memory trace is a frisson of life whereas the monument is a dead crystal-lization. It is *presence* whereas the monument points elsewhere.

The Memory trace is at once collective and individual, vertical and horizontal, communitarian and cosmopolitan, unmovable and mobile, as well as fragile, whereas the monument always bears witness to the entrenched, vertical authority of the dominant power.

The meanings of the Memory trace are constantly evolving, with diffuse ramifications and inter-retro-reactions. The monument has only one single signification that most often fades in one or two generations.

The Memory trace is unfathomable.

The Memory trace might be material, for example the cliff from which the Caribs threw themselves en masse into the ocean to escape slavery. It might be symbolic like the mountain forests where runaway slaves took refuge, or like the silk-cotton tree. It might be functional as in the coolie temple, or in the shack of old Negros, or in *gros ka* drums.

The gestures, the habits, the trades, the silent forms of knowledge, the corporeal forms of knowledge, the instinctive forms of knowledge, the symbols, the emblems, the words, the songs, the Creole language, the landscape, the old trees, the cooperative societies, the cane fields, the quarters—these are the Memory traces that we must now learn to recognize, to catalogue, and to explore with the aim of patiently weaving together the open complexity of our creole patrimonies.

The penal colony of French Guiana is one such example.

The penitentiary of French Guiana is closely linked to the activity of clearing and planting the land as part of colonialism. This penitentiary activity produced these structures and buildings of exploitation (if it is possible here to risk putting it that way). These structures were places of imprisonment, security zones, forest camps, artisan workshops, hangars, forges, zoos, hospitals, and administrative offices. In the shared Imaginary, French Guiana's land was viewed as a protective berm surrounding the prison. Up until 1946, and even after that, to say "French Guiana" meant no more than the "penal colony."

The Guianese, refusing this equation, turned their backs on the remains of the penal colony, and even its very idea. As soon as the penitentiary activity ended, they attempted to forget these places, these walls, these holds, these grilles, these innumerable iron shackles, and these wharves.

They tried to consign the penal colony to oblivion.

The penitentiary architecture is visible beneath the relentless encroachment of the forest. Only the old penal workers have living memories, and their descendants, and their contemporaries. They recount to anyone willing to listen extraordinary stories that I was able to hear for myself at the end of a long chain of echoes. Well, I didn't hear the half of it, but the little that was offered to me reminded me that there was in that location one of the most poignant divagations of humanity.

One of the most repugnant, as well.

In delving into the stories of the penal colony, I found all the heroism, all the dignity, all the fervor, but also all the inhumanity, the aggressive denials, the height of suffering and indignity, the pinnacle of courage and weakness, a mind-boggling concentration of everything that makes up humanity: explosions of shadows and light, of light in shadows, and shadows lightening. All of this is dispersed in the Guianese Memory, pushed to the furthest, dimmest corners of the Guianese mind.

But forgetting sometimes makes you remember.

Forgetting makes you remember because of the rigor of the act of forgetting. And forgetting returns to remembering in another manner: French Guiana forgot the penal colony to remember it better. Because the penal colony was located at the living heart of French Guiana in the same forgotten story of slavery, Amerindian revolt, runaway slaves, gold fever and prospectors, and Chinese settlers. The routes, the paths, the railroads, the land reclamation projects, the construction of buildings, canals, dikes, the connection of villages, the administrative and commercial activity, and the memory of the arts—there wasn't a single space that didn't profit from the industry of the penal worker. There wasn't a single penal worker who didn't give a little of his life, his suffering, his blood, his rage for survival, and his talent for this country.

French Guiana was born from these silent miseries and from these subterranean memories, as well. All of these memories are a part of the country. If even one memory should be missing from the inventories of meaning, then French Guiana wouldn't know how to know itself.

Who could have dared think like this a century ago?

The penitentiary structures of horror, worn down by the years, polished by time, are transformed not into monuments, but into Memory traces. And these vestiges, even though essentially colonial, present the paradox of not bearing witness to colonial domination but to those beneath it who tried to draw in more breaths more full of oxygen—I mean, more humanity.

These remains bear witness to a human tragedy: they make Traces.

The structures of organized death make Memory traces because they arise from death. They return to death the opacity that evokes feeling, that is to say, emotions and flashes of sensations.

They make Memory traces because for many years they were abandoned to a solitary confrontation with vegetal fury, coiling roots, and suffocating branches. The walls had to fight with the tortured tree life rising from their hearts; tree stumps unearthed enormous rocks one by one. Rain, insects, and humidity petrified the wood, wore down iron, stone, grilles, and broke into holds and buildings. People came, rampaged, pillaged, and lived in the desolation.

It could never be wholly effaced.

But the memory of the men who had been there, who had suffered there, was mysteriously still alive. From the wear and tear of this confrontation were borne the most stunning of human patrimonies: the Memory traces of the penal colony of French Guiana.

The Memory traces of the penal colony are broken, diffused, scattered. You can't approach them in the same manner that you do the façade of a Cistercian abbey or a Roman church. I can't, and I don't wish to, give you the official tour, or render for you the spaces and walls in well-planned words. I can't, and I don't wish to, wax eloquently on the balance of height and weight and other architectural features. It's a strictly Western naiveté to think that something lost to time can be elucidated in descriptions of volume, mass, and surface. The monument is indescribable, and it can be imagined only in the exact alchemical moment when it emerges from behind its material conditions. The Memory trace is even more indescribable because it offers little by way of volume and mass. To go there isn't to do something. It's to live as a medium to the beyond.

The Memory traces of the penal colony begin along the ocean, from Cayenne to Saint-Laurent, passing through Kourou. Beginning in 1852,* numerous attempts were made to establish camps after the decision to transport to the colonies all French prisoners condemned to forced labor. Each time, malarial fever wiped out the convicts and their warders. The first camps to find a reprieve were in the breezy islands where the insects and their fever seemed less virulent. What the Amerindians called the Islands of the Devil had become very quickly Salvation's Islands *where it was possible to survive.*

These three islands off the coast of Kourou (Île Royale, Devil's Island, Saint-Joseph Island) were the epicenter of the first penitentiary activity in French Guiana. It's from there that governor after governor, with the dead piling up by the hundreds, set out to establish new camps, new settlements—to overcome obstacles, to attempt audacious new locations very quickly abandoned. They drew inland, along the rivers, to the place at the mouth of the Maroni River that would take the name Saint-Laurent. This is where the penal colony found its center. From there, the forest camps would be established, the artisanal activity, the agricultural work, everything. It was there where the most complete structures were built. It was there where the administration of death set down its rules.

* Decreed March 27, 1852. Put into law May 30, 1854.

But the Memory traces of today don't only bear witness to the history of the penal colony—a fascinating and terrible history. One can find that in dozens of books, chronicles, witness accounts, and celebrated articles. It's better to abjure history writing on the penal colony; then can we discern what the Memory traces murmur to us.

They don't speak only of the penal colony. Through time, they have become charged with countless memories. Today, the long, mossy sighs of Memory traces can be heard within the forest life that seems to encase them. The structure becomes a ruin, and by a spontaneous movement resulting from an invisible accumulation, the ruin becomes open memories.

The idea of departure isn't artistic.

It's wholly utilitarian.

Dangerous men must be incarcerated, they must be made to suffer … and the logic inevitably goes that they must also be eliminated. Their vitality will be sacrificed on the altar of the colonial project—to wit, civilization's inroads in barbarian lands. And, year after year, setback after setback, escape after escape, murderous fury after the delirium of imprisonment, they built, they refined, they improved. Military Engineering and Civil Engineering competed for pride of place. Laterite, iron, chains, wood, earth, construction materials fabricated in France met with the challenge of men who wanted to survive. The point of combustion between life and death, between resistance and oppression, is found in these structures. And, with the passage of time, these tense fibers linking men, linking the survivors and the dead, these interminable sorrows, these suffocating disappointments, these stupors, these fleeting moments of happiness, this life of emergency, began to penetrate the material world: the materials became receptacles of emotion, and sensible antennae. This is a Memory trace.

Structures become ruins, but under the law of sedimentary memory, ruins become artistic combinations. Here, restoration wouldn't make any sense.

The prison at Saint-Laurent du Maroni. The walls there are pale, terrible, scarred by humidity and by successive layers of old paint. The brickwork in its red tints, the earth with its red, hot presence, the moss that clings to everything. It's no longer a question of color. You're facing skin itself.

Transportation Camp.

It's written there. *Transportation. Camp.* Behind these words are rules, regulations, a classification of suffering, a path directed toward death or collapse. What does it matter what the words mean? They're hieroglyphs. They don't mean anything but a kaleidoscopic flash of memories. *Saint-Laurent . . . Devil's Island . . . Saint-Joseph Island . . . Transported . . . Re-incarcerated . . . Deported* . . . each word—each place charts existence in its own way; each word—each place has its penitentiary rhythm; each word—each place has its imprisoned silences; each word—each place has its survival strategies and surveillance laws. What does it matter, their meanings, if the engraved words, if the painted words, scintillate from out of the opaque with a tangible density?

The sun cuts through everything. Saint-Laurent is covered in glare. The caretaker isn't there. It's closed. But it's possible nevertheless to enter into the long courtyard flanked by raised cells. It's as though you are suddenly inside a disemboweled ship that has foundered in the red earth.

Certain places were restored for a film. And these restored places feel like zones of destruction. The original color is there, the original form, but they destroyed the tremulous memories.

Blockhouse . . . Library . . . Disciplinary Quarters . . . Administrative Building . . . Special Section . . . Words divide space. In the chaotic deconstruction of Memory traces, these words indicate places that have lost their initial function and are now suspended in half-fantasy. *Blockhouse* no longer means solitary confinement, silence, stubborn pain held up by the triumphant power, a large, womb-like darkness. It's like a tomb. Entering there, you sit on an iron ring. Rubbing the nape of your neck within the heaviness of the walls, touching the walls' damp skin, is to attempt to experience the place beneath the rounded canopy. The sensation of immobility is immediate. Outside, the hot blade of the sun makes you recoil from the world. You sit in the shade, in its relief, in an envelope of cool. You feel life slow down to a grinding halt, you feel imprisoned in a stone in which there remains but one breath. I have known how to live through these vestiges. I know how to touch them, how to allow their sensations to grow in me. I have seen the slave holds, the sugar mills, the sugar plantation lodgings, the landscapes, and the quarters where suppressed memories may emerge. I find them here, coiled in the solitary confinement of a deserted prison, transfigured beneath the sun into a vast word that, because of its intensity, is frozen in the act of speaking. A cry—sculpted silent on the lips.

In the stark light of the courtyard, the shadows align in squares. Each is an opening more than a cell. In each shadow, traces linger—the reveille at five to the tune of the Diane, the stench of bitter soup, scraps of spongy bread, and the wasting away of despairing bodies in fetid corners. The iron bars cut the odors that the wind brings from the brick factory, from the lime kilns, from the charcoal kilns. Each odor recalls a part of life. It trembles, it attests to the presence of the world.

O, this silence!

It will be there for all eternity. It's there in each stone, it illuminates each angle. Even the wind that ripples the corrugated siding, that wipes the lips of the well, that kicks along the scattered debris, even it will no longer be heard from. Under the law of this place, we surprise ourselves by falling silent. It is as if we begin to watch out for these brusque sounds—emitted in despair—which must have often punctuated this cloak of silence. I conjure you, frenetic hands gripping iron bars. I know you, nails that claw at walls. I sense you, moans that the stone refused to squelch, burbling like stubborn springs. The rust of iron fences was fed by sweat and darkened by many episodes of remembering. The visible bears its trace.

To lean over the well like so many others did, so long ago. The circle of stones remembers this meager ritual. The hole reaches down to the water where heavy shadows merge. The water reflects the stones capping the well. Then your own shadow appears, cast down on the black water. The well seems incongruous. It doesn't quench anyone's thirst. It doesn't seem to function any longer as a well but as a nest of shadows and of angles woven into the depths of the red earth. For what nocturnal hopes does this strange brood exist?

In the islands, certain cells have grille ceilings. A slight curve to the wall protects the sleeper from the rain and sun. The warder saw from his perch the crucified presence in the blackness. The sun slashes the depths of this hole. The decor has remained the same, no more than the presence-absence of a human form that thickens the shadows. (I hear the regular footfall of a boot, sometimes weary, always bored—O, *warder!*)

In the forest camps, the prisoners had to survive grueling labor, fevers, black vomit, food shortages, and the exactions of the guards and wardens. Prisoners had to fight against everyone and everything, and fight against themselves. Horror penetrated everything. This inhumanity was the goal of the administration, and it infected even the function of discipline. The convict and the guard found themselves tied to the same inhalation in which both the excess of desire to survive and the omnipotence of the power to punish led, for one and for the other, to an equal degradation.

The photos of prisoners bear witness to the withering away of men and to the avid fever of their eyes, as though the final energy of the will to live set up its defenses in the fragile liberty of their eyes. We have already seen the same in other camps of despair.

The whip's odor of tar and vinegar, its odor of blood. The brutality of the guaiacum wood used as a handle and a weapon as well. The branding. The rack. The thumbscrew. One had to survive, survive, hug the walls, survive, tame the cages, survive, enter into sad conversation with this shadow, and this wall-skin, and this violent light that surrounded the silhouette of the warder with the sparks of hell. Survive.

Shadows crosshatched with the light, and flashes of the guillotine. These jarring contrasts. They have always been brutal. From the depths of the prison to the prison yard. From the prison yard to the cell. From work to punishment. To emerge from the bitter stillness of the shadows and from its gasps of despair. To emerge into the joy of the light, of the body that unfolds, of others that you can see, touch, to whom you can speak . . . *here, a cigarette!* Then, to return to the shadows with the thrill of the light in your silent stomach. Shadow and lights didn't move, they are there, and, as you move, they speak. A brutal rhythm.

The stomach—the final hold—the only intimacy. The secret double of the walls and the shadows. But intimacy existed only inside the stomach. There they hid their treasures, their money, their tools for escape, their means of survival. Terrible suppository. No blockhouse, no cell, no wall recalls privacy, and that's why no individual presences can be recovered there. They were no more than the secret doubles of a haggard mass rendered into numbers, a milling, ambiguous mass—humanity dehumanized. They returned to their bodies to preserve some measure of an individual life. Only the stomach . . .

Water gives life to walls, pushes breath into bricks. Paint mixes with the moss, and from the smallest crack the call to life brings forth the little green shoots of the forest. They had to be removed. Your life depended on it, your death as well. So in front of this little ghostly landscape, here and there, I can sense it—in this cell, beneath this mossy canopy, on these walkways leading to where the slashes on this wall are found in greatest number, you can stop and think about life. Not life beyond these walls, but life itself. People are better at seeing. Eyes catch out the least detail. And to look is to bring to life. The Transportation Camp is so unsettling, so wrenching, it leads to so many sensations, that it's possible to imagine, even today, the price of a doomed blade of grass that holds to a stone, of lichen that perseveres in the dense shadows. To hold on to. To persevere.

Flesh knows how to wear down stone. In Saint-Laurent, or in the islands, the marks of wear are there to be seen. These broken, rutted walkways, this black that congeals next to the openings, this specific patina that bears witness to an everyday gesture. Flesh is made into sculpture, painting. The rubbing confrontation of human and stone, human and steel, was subtle. Look at the rounded angles, inspect the ferocity of these grilles that remain intact after so many bodies smashed against them. Imagine the alleyways, this square that recalls disciplinary walks enforced with silence and anguish. Look at the marks of wear, look at their absences.

The walls were broken down. Iron rods join cells, barracks, glimpses of the sky, dense shadows. Enormous columns alive to the touch extend down the walkways. In Saint-Laurent, the part of the roof restored for the film registers a logic that is quickly lost in the marks of wear that make memo-ries. *O, the shadows are so old!* In certain places, victims of serial maledictions, light splashes down to render them obsolete. But those that remain are re-enforced and made heavy. And in this dark shadow cut by half-invisible grilles you sense the depths.

In the shadows, try to survive. Cultivate memories of life before arriving here, feel again the little joys, the moments of tenderness, the faces of those you love, a child, a wife, a mother, a friend . . . The shadows make you introspec-tive, they envelope you. It's easy to get accustomed to the shadows, to refuse to leave, to distrust the light, to mistake the warder for the light, condemnation for light. In the Transportation Camp, just as on each of Salvation's Islands, you have to stop in these shadows and wait to bear witness to the morbid collusion of prisoner and shadows.

Certain prisoners didn't want to look inside themselves. There was nothing good inside, they had only the desire to forget and to abandon the past. For them, shadows were abhorrent. They wanted to cast them off. They raged and shouted, they cried for light. The fresh, damp shadows that I find here recall these tears.

Yes, the shadows were accommodating, but not always the light. In the camps, the shadows were tamed by the desire to live. They covered up heinous and silent deaths, and unthinkable atrocities, but they also assuaged childish bewilderment, long and bitter reveries, and revolts. The light intensified the submission of the forced marches, it weighed on the shoulders, bent backs beneath straw hats; the ground, sprouting new growth, already damp despite the harsh sun, was the only thing seen by these men who walked with bowed heads and broken spirits.

In Salvation's Islands, the obsessive attempt to see beyond the stones to the presence of the sea, its roar that isolates and that connects, that imprisons and that, day after day, promises the chance of leaving.

I walk through the hangars, the corrugated iron rent with holes, the ruined walls, the jaws of cells. I see the metallic frames encaging hollow spaces, I see the years scratched into the walls, and everywhere the green velour of the lichen. I pause where shadows and light form a sculpture whose former meaning is unmasked. Who came here? What happened here? This place of horror? This place of pacification? There's no way to know now. We don't understand much of it anymore. We can only perceive these presences and their shattered meanings. Each piece of debris seems to participate in a balance whose law would be disorder and chaos. The place lives with the sun that moves. Silence flows from the power of the sun and doubles in the shadows.

Rings and figures. Holes. Grilles. What does this number 26 here mean? What, this 25? Some are effaced, some remain. The figures combine with drawings, with scratches, with black moss; they cover the skin of the wall with their disturbing tattoos. No names, no addresses: just figures. A figuring of spaces, uses, functions. Despite myself, I count them out silently, one after another, 22, 23, 25, 27 — they resound in my head like a response to the silence, a response more vertical than these grilles, more vertical than a ray of sun that disappears suddenly on a shadow's edge.

Walking with a bowed head, I meet other glances out of the corner of my eye. The ceilings are far away, infrequently noticed. An infectious leprosy spreads. The stones move, creating fissures. What point would there have been to look into the sky, when survival in the bellies of the camps, in the barricades of the islands, happened only on the ground? And the ground witnesses this: the earth, the stones, the cement — the ground was the friend to many human wreckages. How many tended gardens like a person pokes at a dying fire? Don't die here.

Tuberculosis.
Dysentery.
Scurvy.
Stomach ailments.
Hauling these trees till nightfall.
Used up.

Don't die here.
The ocean and the rivers are vast cemeteries. Only Memory traces know precisely, secretly, the exact count of those who died here.

For the homeless, a Memory trace is welcoming. They live in the cells. We use one as a resting place. Others take up residence there. Some little chairs, a television, and some flowers don't seem out of place. Chickens walk around. There are plastic tubs, paint cans used to catch rainwater. There is no wastage: with their few things, they build a delicate hope that resembles those of the most serene prisoners. But this time, the doors with their peepholes remain open as though fearing that the jaws would clang shut upon a stifled cry. Now laundry dries.

Night in the common-house. We're seated on the stone floor, in this rattling of chains that follows our movements. Smoking. The reddening in the shadows. And this sharing of the cigarette, and the cockroach that flits after the cigarette circulating from man to man. The ocean beats against the night.

The door is torn open. It's set against the wall. Its metal force, suddenly, is useless. Rust gives it a mottled hide. Bars, nails, giant locks, mechanisms of imprisonment, veer toward new meanings. It becomes a sort of metal sculpture that lengthens the skin of the walls, matching the marks of wear. The door squelched so much vitality, denied so many hopes, trapped so many shadows that from now on, due to the door being wrenched open, it's part of the camp that has become a Memory trace.

Doors of thick wood, iron. Enormous latches. Peepholes. Locks pried off, taken for some other use. The rusted iron leeched into the wood, tattooing the stones. The marks of wear evince a painstaking patience.

Transportation Camp. The shutters open onto memories. The film, there again, with its brightly colored banners. Who ripples them today with gusts of wind?

And the hospital? A haven amidst the pain of all the camps. To take advantage of them, it was often necessary to have more than courage. Someone decides to mutilate himself. Someone comes with a wad of spit in his mouth saying it's tuberculosis. He pays dearly for this spit (a weak purulence) in front of the doctor's bored suspicion. Someone gives himself leprosy and waits for seven years. What does it matter if death comes, if the joy of liberation is impeccable. And Implacable.

Enormous roots have long since grown over the walls. We see their parasitic growths scarring the walls, pulling inconceivable lifeblood from stones and cement—the sap of what couldn't be extracted from hearts and souls. I saw the same in Louisiana. Plantation owners had thrown the corpses of spent slaves into the middle of a vast field. Over the course of time, trees with twisted branches grew in this crude cemetery, which seemed to moan during the harvests. In the Transportation Camp and on the islands, the walls expel from the dungeons of their shadows a mysterious energy that the plant life absorbs.

In the shadows of the cell, the light falls through the crisscross of the grille. Square, rectangle, and half moon. It's not only the light that the grille disturbs, but also the wind, the odors, the patches of sky, the parts of walls, the patches of still life. And the grille mirrors life: it makes a painting in which you no longer believe. Your eyes lift only by reflex. The grille transforms life into an image whose meaning quickly recedes from view. The passage of the sun overhead makes an illusory movement; the shadows, lighter here, darker there, shift imperceptibly. The cell lightens minute by minute, the depths remain the depths, the lines of the grille lengthen, shorten, then disappear in the reddish clarity that hesitates at the edge of the black pit of the agony of imprisonment. The night is frightening.

The night is frightening. The iron is colder. The stone is damper. Wood is no one's friend. And the assault of the shadows numbs the soul.

The Church of Saint-Joseph of Iracoubo—a vow of happiness in the midst of a permanent dream—another quality of silence. The solemnity is feverish in the painter Huguet's impressive admixture of colors—the painter, a prisoner who in order to survive clung to his brushes for eight years. He covered everything in a giant fresco—the ceiling, nave, choir, chevet, pillars. Huguet took refuge in the very tip of his brush, he made everything so small, so minute, against a background of light blue. He marked his existence in thousands of flowers that transport you through a sparkling, stationary hypnosis. He imagined himself in virgins, saints, little stoic angels covered in hefty garlands, Hic Est Domus Dei . . . His miniature, worrisome half-life exploded here in a generous cry. What was your vow, O dream?

Four stairs lead to the Blockhouse. There's no longer a door. Only the welcome of an intense night that seems to open into a black chasm, an abyss, of what helplessness. And each footfall resounds on the stones broken in their center so long ago that they seem to crack again beneath the hesitant footfall. The number above the opening announces nothing that gives credence to numbers. Everything begins and ends with supplication.

Like prosthetic limbs, iron joints punctuate the living skin of the walls. Hinges. Rings. Rectangular or square panels. Nails. An encrustation of rust makes a second skin. A part of the dark paint that covers the bottom of the wall is diluted by the light paint that covers the top. Moss, lichen, scratches, dampness, earth, dust compose a strange canvas that you can inspect in the frame of your hands. And the abstraction conveys the unknown properties of these mixed colors. Acid and heat. The perfume of earth: the colors speak.

These broken walls, these remnants of the walkways, these iron roofs marred with holes, these tombs, these collapsed stones, these dead lawns that carpet the ground, all of it recalls elementary forms and the reverberations of these elemental forms: squares, circles, triangles, straight and curved lines, trapezoids, and their infinite conjunctions. The functional and the abstract, what is recognizable and what is unrecognizable, what is immediately clear and what must be conjured, a primordial broth, a chaotic harmony whose first constant remains the emotion of the penal colony's memory. The marks of wear that recall abandonment fix these parts according to an imperceptible—but dominant—aesthetic of internal necessity.

Reverberations come from everywhere, from color, material, stone, iron, shadows, explosions of light. They stand apart, or they meld in points of confluence that I discover as I wander. Here, nothing is measured, but all is rhythm. Measurement is for a reading of what is made. The Memory trace arises from marks of wear and the chaotic destruction of buildings, matter, and meaning. They emerge through rhythm.

When I retrace my steps, nothing is the same, the lights and the shadows have changed, other details appear, other things seem important, other odors and other sensations are emitted from the colors, everything is alive and calls to the spirit. The plea is eternal. Each inspection surprises anew.

In the sections of the walls with gaping wounds (thresholds without doors, windows without shutters, breaches . . .), you see appear, confusingly, bits of sky, branches, tree trunks, leaves. The wall's presence proposes through its first principle the framing of this destruction; and what is made comprehensible in this way then catapults you toward an abstraction that forces you to feel deeply.

⤛※⤜

From the earthen carpet, the walls rise up with decadent pride. Looking down the wall, you follow the wall's height, and in the unforeseen interruption of a branch, the dilapidation of the wall's crest transforms it into a troubling stele.

⤛※⤜

And so here I am in the Memory traces of the penal colony of French Guiana, not as a visitor but as a wanderer, not strolling but circling through detours. I don't enter the front door to leave by the rear. I follow a desire for an impossible totality that I can only faintly perceive. That each part holds the whole, and that the feeling of the whole remains possible in the hints of parts. The walls that are no longer walls, the hinges that hang like questions, the windows that breathe, the walls that no longer enclose anything, the fittings that are suddenly strange . . . Forget the old words. New ones are necessary. All these first meanings are pushed into a tension that trembles and torques, a sort of unraveling that the divagation of my steps and spirit produce.

I am ready to feel.

Presence brings out emotion.

⤛※⤜

And I see that I would never be able to write, never be able to capture in a single phrase, these Memory traces. After I leave, oral storytellers with grave voices, *tambouyé* drummers, jazz musicians, blues singers, *bel-air* call-and-response singers, guitar players, dancers whose bodies billow and stretch

will have to be called on. In order for this concert to transmit some sense
of the penal colony's formidable abstraction, photographers, sculptors, and
artists gifted with color will be necessary. This is how it will be possible to
stop the erosion of these Memory traces, and to give them life.

When do eroding memories crumble for good?
How are we to recognize this limit?
Where are we to place it?
How are we to stabilize it?

In every possible way, we must work to stop the wearing down and to begin
a conservation process of what remains. And for this, we must cast away the
renovators, step aside from those hoping to reconstruct, send from these
places the builders and architects, the industrialists of tourism, and the
politician-developers. We must give over these fragile memories not to the
keepers of monuments, but to those who since the beginning of time have
known how to take care of the Memory traces of the world: the friends of
silence, the brothers of solitude, the allies of the mineral, the terrifying souls
who listen to what no one any longer hears—those who leave behind in their
untamed passage the pastures of invisible memories.

Here, the conservator will be one with the poets.
And the conservation will be a poetics.
I leave French Guiana in somber spirits, my heart possessed.

Cayenne, La Favorite, December 7, 1993

It seemed to me that I was in a strange cemetery and that I was going to place, not flowers, but a packet of tobacco on each tomb.

Albert Londres, *Au bagne*

Kourou, Devil's Island. Alfred Dreyfus's house. Cell window.
Classified as a national historical monument (CLMH) on December 30, 1987.

Alfred Dreyfus's house.

Île Royale. House of the prison director.
Classified as a regional historical monument (ISMH) on February 25, 1986.

Île Royale. Cell block entrance.

Île Royale. Cell block. ISMH: February 25, 1986.

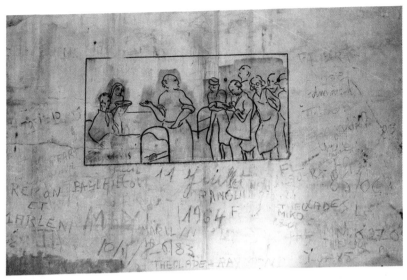

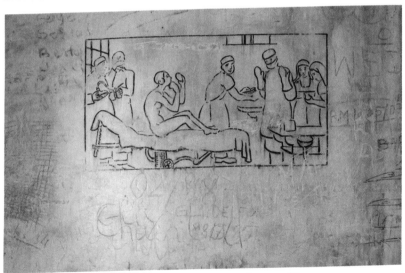

Murals attributed to Francis Lagrange, the counterfeiter.

Île Royale. Military hospital. CLMH: August 5, 1980.

Île Royale. Bakery.

Île Royale. Mental hospital ruins.

Île Royale. Building of the Saint-Paul Sisters of Chartres. Maternity ward.

Île Royale. Children's cemetery.

Saint-Laurent du Maroni. Saint-Jean Prison Camp. Prison warden cemetery.

Saint-Jean Prison Camp. Chapel basement.

Montsinéry-Tonnegrande. Crique Anguille Prison Camp for the Vietnamese. Cells.

Crique Anguille Prison Camp for the Vietnamese. Cell interior.

Mana. Coswine Prison Camp. Remains of an oven.

Saint-Laurent du Maroni. Forestière Prison Camp.

Saint-Laurent du Maroni. Prisoner wharf.

Saint-Laurent du Maroni. Transportation Camp.
Freemen quarters, view over cell roofs. CLMH: August 26, 1987.

Transportation Camp.

Transportation Camp. Building interior.

Transportation Camp. Freemen quarters, view over courtyard.

Transportation Camp. Solitary confinement.

Transportation Camp. Solitary confinement.

"Blockhouse . . . Library . . . Disciplinary Quarters . . .
Administrative Building . . . Special Section . . . *Words divide space.*"

Transportation Camp. Freemen quarters.

Transportation Camp.

Transportation Camp. Freemen quarters. Library.

Transportation Camp. Disciplinary quarters.

Transportation Camp. Entrance to solitary confinement.

Transportation Camp. Entrance to disciplinary quarters.

Transportation Camp. Freemen quarters.

Transportation Camp. Cell interior.

Transportation Camp. Freemen quarters.

Transportation Camp. Solitary confinement. Cell 47, Charière's cell.

Transportation Camp. Solitary confinement. Cell floor corner.

Transportation Camp. Convict quarters. Well wheel.

Transportation Camp. Solitary confinement. Guillotine site, kitchens in the rear.

"Transportation. Camp. Behind these words are rules, regulations,
a classification of suffering, a path directed toward death or collapse."

Iracoubo. Church of Saint-Joseph.
Murals painted by the convict Pierre Huguet. CLMH: June 8, 1978.

Church of Saint-Joseph. Choir and main altar.

Church of Saint-Joseph. Ceiling.

Saint-Joseph Island. Road to Point Isabelle.

Saint-Joseph Island. Penitentiary. Disciplinary quarters.

Saint-Joseph. Penitentiary. Canteen.

Saint-Joseph Island. Penitentiary. Entrance to the disciplinary quarters.

Saint-Joseph Island. Penitentiary interior.

Saint-Joseph Island. Penitentiary. Disciplinary quarters.

"We see their parasitic growths scarring the walls,
pulling inconceivable lifeblood from stones and cement . . ."

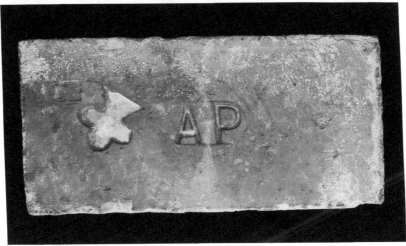

Bricks made by convicts. The stamp "AP" means "administration pénitentiaire."

Kourou. Semaphore telegraph tower called Dreyfus Tower.

In memory of Icek Baron.

About the Contributors

The author, PATRICK CHAMOISEAU, was born in 1953 in Martinique and has become one of the island's most successful and celebrated authors. Chamoiseau has written autobiographical narratives, assembled a collection of folktales, and been at the forefront of the theoretical debates surrounding *créolité*, or creoleness. He is the author of numerous books in French, including fiction, long essays, comics, a play, and a children's book. His novels include *Chronique des sept misères*, *Solibo Magnifique*, and *Texaco*, which won the Prix Goncourt in 1992. As author, poet, and critical theorist, Chamoiseau continues to be one of the most important and creatively provocative voices in Caribbean and world literature.

The translator, MATT REECK, has published five translations from the French and the Urdu. His work has been supported by grants from the Fulbright Foundation, the National Endowment for the Arts, and the PEN/Heim Fund.

The photographer, RODOLPHE HAMMADI, is an award-winning French photojournalist, photographer, and sculptor. As a photojournalist, he has won the "Villa Médicis" for his work in the 5th Centenary of Brazil, and the Leonardo da Vinci Award for a photo report on Yemen. His photographs have been featured in the Centre Georges Pompidou, the Gérald Piltzer gallery, and the Musée Carnavale. His current project is a series of sculptures called "Mes Armes."

CHARLES FORSDICK is James Barrow Professor of French at the University of Liverpool. He has published widely on colonial history, postcolonial literature, the cultures of slavery, and travel writing.